May you always be known for the LOVE you give and the CARE you show to the friends who surround you.

Dear friends, let us continue to love one another, for love comes from God. Anyone who loves is a child of God and knows God.

1 JOHN 4:7 NLT

For one human being to love another: that is the work for which all other work
is

RA

MW01493834

DaySpring

I will **pray** for you
for as long as you need,
in any way you need,
with **love** and **faith**
that it will all work out
for the good.

Don't worry about anything; instead,
pray about everything. Tell God what you need,
and thank Him for all He has done.
Philippians 4:6 NLT

The gift of friendship among women
is a treasure not to be taken lightly.
Women friends become the face of God
to one another—the face of grace,
of delight, of mercy.

STASI ELDREDGE

I'm asking God
to give you
ENCOURAGEMENT
so deep it will
never run out.

*Encourage each other and build each other
up, just as you are already doing.*

I THESSALONIANS 5:11 NLT

Encouragement is awesome. It has the capacity
to lift a man's or woman's shoulders....
To breathe fresh fire into the fading embers
of a smoldering dream. To actually change
the course of another human being's day,
week, or life.

Charles Swindoll

You are so great at just being with people. I am praying God will SHINE through you with a BRILLIANCE that lightens the darkness of others.

Let your light shine for all to see. For the glory of the Lord rises to shine on you.

Isaiah 60:1 NLT

Begin today! No matter how feeble the light, let it shine as best it may. The world may need just that quality of light which you have.

HENRY C. BLINN

DaySpring

God made you with a
beautiful smile, a laugh
that lights up the room,
and a kind heart
that cares for others.
I'm thanking Him for you!

*So let us come boldly to the throne
of our gracious God. There we will receive
His mercy, and we will find grace
to help us when we need it most.*

HEBREWS 4:16 NLT

You are valuable just because you exist.
Not because of what you do or what
you have done, but simply because you are.

MAX LUCADO

DaySpring

I am **trusting** God will never send you down the wrong path. I'm **trusting** Him with you and for you!

The LORD says, "I will guide you along
the best pathway for your life.
I will advise you and watch over you."

PSALM 32:8 NLT

Whether we are poets or parents or teachers
or artists or gardeners, we must start
where we are and use what we have.
In the process of creation and relationship,
what seems mundane and trivial
may show itself to be holy,
precious part of a pattern.

Luci Shaw

Your LOVE for others is an EXAMPLE for all. I'm praising God for you, friend.

You are far more valuable to Him than any birds!

LUKE 12:24 NLT

Caring and loving must be verbalized if you are going to be a friend. Your spoken expressions of care will build a strong bridge.

JIM CONWAY

DaySpring

Thanking God for who He made you to be, and that no matter how different our lives may be, you are **always** a true friend.

For when we ourselves are comforted, we will certainly comfort you. Then you can patiently endure the same things we suffer.

II Corinthians 1:6 NLT

The most beautiful discovery true friends make is that they can grow separately without growing apart.

ELISABETH FOLEY

In times like these—
there is **PEACE**,
there is **HOPE**,
there is **FAITH**,
there is **JESUS**.
Praying for you.

*The only thing that counts
is faith expressing itself through love.*

GALATIANS 5:6 NIV

God created human beings in His image
so they can be friends—intimate,
love-filled companions—with Him
and one another.

John Ortberg

DaySpring

Whatever you need— GOD IS. I am asking Him to show you all the POSSIBILITIES for overcoming today!

Love never gives up, never loses faith, is always hopeful, and endures through every circumstance.

I Corinthians 13:7 NLT

Every day we live is a priceless gift of God, loaded with possibilities to learn something new, to gain fresh insights.

DALE EVANS ROGERS

Just wanted you
to know that your inner
grace and beauty
continually bless me!
I pray that you are blessed
continually today.

*Let us try to do what makes peace
and helps one another.*

ROMANS 14:19 NCV

Notice words of compassion.
Seek out deeds of kindness. These are like
the doves from heaven, pointing out
to you who are the ones blessed
with inner grace and beauty.

CHRISTOPHER DE VINCK

Praying that the God of
miracles overwhelms you
with His incredible **love**
so that it bubbles over
onto your friends and family.

*Encourage one another and build each other up,
just as in fact you are doing.*

I THESSALONIANS 5:11 NIV

We never live so intensely
as when we love strongly.
We never realize ourselves so vividly
as when we are in the full glow
of love for others.

Walter Rauschenbusch

I pray that the JOYS of today will be more than your HEART can contain, bringing a SMILE to your face that others can't help but notice.

What a relief to see your friendly smile. It is like seeing the face of God!

GENESIS 33:10 NLT

One of the most important responsibilities in the Christian life is to care about others, smile at them, and be a friend to the friendless.

JAMES DOBSON

You and Jesus, hand in hand, make an **amazing**, unstoppable duo. I'm praying that your **partnership** is revealed in your beautiful spirit!

You should clothe yourselves instead with the beauty that comes from within, the unfading beauty of a gentle and quiet spirit, which is so precious to God.

1 Peter 3:4 NLT

A keen sense of humor helps us to overlook the unbecoming, understand the unconventional, tolerate the unpleasant, overcome the unexpected, and outlast the unbearable.

BILLY GRAHAM

You are going to **MAKE IT THROUGH THIS** because of who you are and whose you are. Standing with you, praying for you.

See how very much our Father loves us,
for He calls us His children,
and that is what we are!

1 JOHN 3:1 NLT

We encounter God in the ordinariness of life, not in the search for spiritual highs and extraordinary, mystical experiences but in our simple presence in life.

Brennan Manning

So thankful my life has been seasoned by your FRIENDSHIP. I'm praying every morning you know how SPECIAL you are.

The steadfast love of the LORD never ceases, His mercies never come to an end; they are new every morning; great is Your faithfulness.

Lamentations 3:22-23 NRSV

We read more deeply, remember more clearly, enjoy events with greater pleasure if we have a friend to share with.

PAM BROWN

Sending up prayers of hope
for you—and waiting to see
the amazing things
God will do with all the little
details of your life!

Above all, clothe yourselves with love,
which binds everything together
in perfect harmony.
COLOSSIANS 3:14 NRSV

I have never been a millionaire. But I have
enjoyed a crackling fire, a glorious sunset,
a walk with a friend.... There are plenty
of life's tiny delights for all of us.

JACK ANTHONY

I pray God will bless our **friendship**, so that we have a safe place to be our true selves for years to come.

I have called you friends, for everything that I learned from my Father I have made known to you.

JOHN 15:15 NIV

Who but a good friend would put her life on hold in order to listen, advise, sympathize, and send you on your way secure in the knowledge that someone cares?

Lois Wyse

You are truly BEAUTIFUL and AMAZING, and I'm praying you know it deeply today!

I pray that your love will overflow more and more, and that you will keep on growing in knowledge and understanding.

PHILIPPIANS 1:9 NLT

Something deep in all of us yearns for God's beauty, and we can find it no matter where we are.

SUE MONK KIDD

You are a shining example of **loyalty** and **truth**. I am thanking God for you!

Greater love has no one than this, that someone lay down his life for his friends. You are my friends if you do what I command.

John 15:13-14 ESV

Whoever walks toward God one step, God runs toward him two.

JEWISH PROVERB

DaySpring

I'm asking Jesus to bring you into HIS REST today.

You see me when I travel and when I rest at home. You know everything I do.

PSALM 139:3 NLT

This is and has been the Father's work from the beginning—to bring us into the home of His heart.

George MacDonald

It's a sure thing,
when GOD is with you,
that things will turn out
for the GOOD.
Praying you take
the time to soak it in!

I have loved you with an everlasting love;
therefore I have continued
My faithfulness to you.

Jeremiah 31:3 NRSV

*What we lack is not so much leisure to do
as time to reflect and time to feel. What we
seldom "take" is time to experience the things
that have happened, the things that are
happening, the things that are still ahead of us.*

MARGARET MEAD AND RHODA METRAUX

Stepping confidently **into the unknown** is what we call big faith! Way to go—I'm praying for your adventure.

You saw me before I was born. Every day of my life was recorded in Your book. Every moment was laid out before a single day had passed. How precious are Your thoughts about me, O God. They cannot be numbered!

PSALM 139:16-17 NLT

Friends are angels who lift our feet when our own wings have trouble remembering how to fly.

ANONYMOUS

DaySpring

Relationships can be tough but so rewarding when God is at the center. Asking Him to always be the center of our friendship.

Perfume and incense bring joy to the heart, and the pleasantness of a friend springs from their heartfelt advice.

PROVERBS 27:9 NIV

Time alone with God can help us grow, but so can serving others.

Keri Wyatt Kent

Every MORNING as you begin your day, REMEMBER that I'm praying for you. Our FRIENDSHIP is very important.

Love each other deeply
with all your heart.
1 PETER 1:22 NLT

Friendship is usually treated by the majority of mankind as a tough and everlasting thing which will survive all manner of bad treatment. But...its conditions of existence are that it should be dealt with delicately and tenderly being as it is a sensitive plant and not a roadside thistle.

OUIDA

Praying for you as you make the hard decisions and trust **God** in big ways. I believe you will fly!

The LORD is gracious and merciful, slow to anger and abounding in steadfast love. The LORD is good to all, and His compassion is over all that He has made.

Psalm 145:8-9 NRSV

When you come to the edge of all the light you have and must take a step into the darkness of the unknown, believe that one of two things will happen. Either there will be something solid for you to stand on— or you will be taught how to fly.

PATRICK OVERTON

May today be surprisingly full OF GOD'S FAITHFULNESS and strength in your life.

The LORD your God is with you....
He will take great delight in you;
in His love He will no longer rebuke you,
but will rejoice over you with singing.

ZEPHANIAH 3:17 NIV

I have never known anyone who succeeded
at relationships—who cultivated
great friendships, who was devoted to his
or her family, who mastered the art of giving
and receiving love—yet had a bad life.

John Ortberg

DaySpring

May you always know
the IMPACT you've had
on the WORLD
around you—
and especially on ME.

There are "friends" who destroy
each other, but a real friend
sticks closer than a brother.
Proverbs 18:24 NLT

*Whatever leisure time we are able to invest
in relationships is time well spent.*
CHARLES SWINDOLL

My favorite thing about you
is the way you reflect Jesus.
Praying that reflection
grows brighter
every day!

I thank my God every time I remember you.
In all my prayers for all of you,
I always pray with joy.

PHILIPPIANS 1:3-4 NIV

Every single act of love
bears the imprint of God.

ANONYMOUS

DaySpring

**Everyday miracles
are God's specialty.
Your light is a miracle to me.
I am keeping you in prayer.**

*I will send down showers in season;
there will be showers of blessing.*

EZEKIEL 34:26 NIV

When you are in the dark, listen, and God
will give you a very precious message
for someone else when you get
into the light.

Oswald Chambers

You can count on me to PRAY even when you don't have the words to ask...and you can count on Jesus to ANSWER.

We don't know what God wants us to pray for. But the Holy Spirit prays for us with groanings that cannot be expressed in words.

Romans 8:26 NLT

Silences make the real conversations between friends. Not the saying but the never needing to say is what counts.

MARGARET LEE RUNBECK

You make a DIFFERENCE—you really do! Praying God makes this so clear to you.

Plant your seed in the morning and keep busy all afternoon, for you don't know if profit will come from one activity or another—or maybe both.

ECCLESIASTES 11:6 NLT

We were created to draw life and nourishment from one another the way the roots of an oak tree draw life from the soil. Community— living in vital connectedness with others— is essential to human life.

John Ortberg

DaySpring

My prayer for you today is that you know your WORTH, live with JOY, and feel the COMPANIONSHIP of God's presence.

Teach us to realize the brevity of life, so that we may grow in wisdom.

Psalm 90:12 NLT

God came to us because God wanted to join us on the road, to listen to our story, and to help us realize that we are not walking in circles but moving toward the house of peace and joy.

HENRI J. M. NOUWEN

It's a great big world out there, and God **is leading you** through it beautifully. Keep smiling and concentrating on the important things— and I'll keep praying!

Above all else, guard your heart, for everything you do flows from it.

PROVERBS 4:23 NIV

The ability to simplify means to eliminate the unnecessary so that the necessary may speak.

HANS HOFMANN

DaySpring

Every day is a fresh start, a new chance, a great time to hope in big ways. I'm asking God to overwhelm you with courage today!

How precious are your thoughts about me, O God. They cannot be numbered! I can't even count them; they outnumber the grains of sand! And when I wake up, you are still with me!

PSALM 139:17–18 NLT

You have an instrument and a song, and you owe it to God to play them both sublimely.

Max Lucado

This isn't an easy time, but God brought us together for a reason. I am behind you all the way! Praying for His PEACE and STRENGTH to encourage you today.

You are joined together with peace through the Spirit, so make every effort to continue together in this way.

EPHESIANS 4:3 NCV

True love possesses the ability to see beyond.... It sees beneath the veneer. Love focuses on the soul. Love sees another's soul in great need of help and sets compassion to work.

CHARLES SWINDOLL

Some people make amazing friends, and I know that means God has poured His **grace** into them. Your **kindness** and **sweetness** are prime examples of that! I am asking Him to keep the grace coming!

Kind words are like honey—
sweet to the soul and healthy for the body.
Proverbs 16:24 NLT

You can make more friends in two months by becoming interested in other people than you can in two years by trying to get other people interested in you.

DALE CARNEGIE

In the big and the
small things, the great
and tender things,
I AM PRAYING
you'll see God's
unchanging love
for you.

*I will gladly spend myself
and all I have for you.*

II CORINTHIANS 12:15 NLT

There never was any heart truly great
and generous that was not also
tender and compassionate.

Robert South

God makes BEAUTIFUL relationships. I am trusting Him with our FRIENDSHIP and praying that He guards it always.

Be kind to one another, tenderhearted, forgiving one another, as God in Christ has forgiven you.
Ephesians 4:32 NRSV

Walk and talk and work and laugh with your friends, but behind the scenes, keep up the life of simple prayer and inward worship.
THOMAS R. KELLY

It's so good to know that
the Lord is with you
right now...taking care
of the details, loving you
with all His heart. I stand
with you and pray with
confidence for your future!

I pray that God, the source of hope,
will fill you completely with joy and peace
because you trust in Him. Then you
will overflow with confident hope
through the power of the Holy Spirit.

ROMANS 15:13 NLT

Indeed, we do not really live unless we have
friends surrounding us like a firm wall
against the winds of the world.

CHARLES HANSON TOWNE

Just in case you're
wondering today —
you're amazing!
I am asking God to remind
you that your gifts
are just the thing so many
of us desperately need.

Let love be your highest goal!
I CORINTHIANS 14:1 NLT

C. S. Lewis once surmised that each person
is created to see a different facet of God's
beauty—something no one else can see
in quite the same way—and then to bless all
worshipers through all eternity with an aspect
of God they could not otherwise see.

JOHN ORTBERG

You're totally not alone.
How do I know? Because
you're on my **heart** and
in my **prayers** so often.
And I know you are
on God's heart too.

May the LORD keep watch between you and me
when we are away from each other.

GENESIS 31:49 NIV

It is an awesome, challenging thought:
The Lord comes to us in our friends.
What we do and are to them is an
expression of what we are to Him.

Lloyd John Ogilvie

DaySpring

Each NEW day is a chance to do one SMALL thing. I've asked God to change the WORLD one small thing at a time through you today!

Be like-minded, be sympathetic, love one another, be compassionate and humble.

1 PETER 3:8 NIV

God's heart is the most sensitive and tender of all. No act goes unnoticed, no matter how insignificant or small.

RICHARD J. FOSTER

Asking **GOD** to remind you that even if you have said the wrong thing, He has new **mercies** for you each day. He will faithfully meet all your needs, He will **always** be with you, and with Him all things are possible.

You must understand this, my beloved: let everyone be quick to listen, slow to speak, slow to anger.

James 1:19 NRSV

Talking comes by nature, silence by wisdom.

AMERICAN PROVERB

No need to worry.
No need to fret.
GOD'S GOT THIS!

*Give all your worries and cares to God,
for He cares about you.*

1 PETER 5:7 NLT

Blessed are they who tenderly seek
to comfort another and never run out
of compassion and grace.

Janet L. Weaver Smith

Today I pray that
EVERY step you take is a
step in God's direction!
And I thank God for
your COMPANIONSHIP
on this path of mine.

His eyes are on the ways of mortals;
He sees their every step.

Job 34:21 NIV

*We have a price to pay for depth in sharing
in another's life. And the one payment
that will yield the greatest interest
is time together.*

JACK MAYHALL

Tough times call for
good friends.
I'm here for you
and praying for your light
to shine brightly.
You can count on me.

A friend loves at all times.
PROVERBS 17:17 NIV

There is not enough darkness in all the world
to put out the light of one small candle...
any reminder of something deeply felt
or dearly loved. No [one] is so poor as not to
have many of these small candles.
When they are lighted, darkness goes away
and a touch of wonder remains.

ARTHUR GORDON

This world needs more people like you, my friend, people who **follow** Jesus and **love** so well. My prayer today is full of **gratitude** for your trusting heart.

These are the things that you shall do: Speak the truth to one another, render... judgments that are true and make for peace.

ZECHARIAH 8:16 NRSV

When God gives a friend, He is entrusting us with the care of another's heart. It is a chance to be a Life giver.

Stasi Eldredge

DaySpring

One day at a time is still never easy, but you've DEFINITELY got what it takes to come through this STRONGER than ever. God has you. Praying for you!

"For the mountains may move and the hills disappear, but even then My faithful love for you will remain. My covenant of blessing will never be broken," says the LORD, who has mercy on you.

ISAIAH 54:10 NLT

To think seldom of your enemies, often of your friends, and every day of Christ; and to spend as much time as you can, with body and with spirit, in God's out-of-doors—these are little guideposts on the footpath to peace.

HENRY VAN DYKE

It's a good day to have a good day. I'm **praying** God weaves threads of **encouragement** and **friendship** into a really good day for you!

May...Christ Himself and God our Father, who loved us and by His grace gave us eternal encouragement and good hope, encourage your hearts and strengthen you in every good deed and word.

II Thessalonians 2:16-17 NIV

There is in friendship something of all relations, and something above them all. It is the golden thread that ties the hearts of all the world.

JOHN EVELYN

I thank God for your forgiving and GRACEFUL SPIRIT. I pray our friendship grows stronger each day.

I have called you friends, for everything that I learned from my Father I have made known to you.

JOHN 15:15 NIV

Who but a good friend would put her life on hold in order to listen, advise, sympathize, and send you on your way secure in the knowledge that someone cares?

Lois Wyse

God is the best kind of companion, confidant, and friend. I'm praying He shows every side of His LOVE for you today and that you are able to share His LOVE with others.

No eye has seen, nor ear heard, nor the human heart conceived, what God has prepared for those who love Him.

I Corinthians 2:9 NRSV

Love is the true means by which the world is enjoyed: our love to others, and others' love to us.

THOMAS TRAHERNE

I'm so proud of you for **working so hard.** And I'm asking God to help you enjoy every step of the process.

But even the hairs of your head are all counted. Do not be afraid; you are of more value than many sparrows.

LUKE 12:7 NRSV

A true friend is one who is concerned about what we are becoming, who sees beyond the present relationship, and who cares deeply about us as a whole person.

GLORIA GAITHER

DaySpring

It's not always easy,
but I **know** you've got this.
Praying you **feel** the Lord
helping you and that His
peace guards your heart.

*And the peace of God, which transcends
all understanding, will guard your hearts
and your minds in Christ Jesus.*

PHILIPPIANS 4:7 NIV

Love to me is when you walk out
on that "one more thing" and say,
"Nothing will come between you and me.
Not even one thing."

Sara Groves

May the process of GROWTH be full of JOY for you—and may you experience His CLOSENESS all the way through from beginning to end.

"For I know the plans I have for you," declares the LORD, "plans to prosper you and not to harm you, plans to give you hope and a future."

JEREMIAH 29:11 NIV

A good friend is a connection to life— a tie to the past, a road to the future.

LOIS WYSE

I thank God for you.
I pray He **blesses** you
and gives you the **gift**
of eternal **love**
and **friendship**.

God so loved the world that He gave
His one and only Son, that whoever believes in Him
shall not perish but have eternal life.

John 3:16 NIV

True friendships are lasting because true love
is eternal. A friendship in which heart speaks
to heart is a gift from God, and no gift that
comes from God is temporary or occasional.

HENRI J. M. NOUWEN

May God bless you
OVER AND OVER
for the ways
you serve and love!

Let us not become weary in doing good,
for at the proper time we will reap
a harvest if we do not give up.
Therefore, as we have opportunity,
let us do good to all people.

GALATIANS 6:9–10 NIV

Great acts of love are done by those who are
habitually performing small acts of kindness.

Anonymous

Praising God today for His FAITHFULNESS toward you! Praising Him for your FRIENDSHIP.

For the LORD is good and His love endures forever; His faithfulness continues through all generations.

Psalm 100:5 NIV

A true friend is the gift of God, and... only He who made hearts can unite them.

ROBERT SOUTH

I know that when you
go through things with God,
you'll come out **stronger,
smarter, better.**
Praying for you!

*Those who hope in the LORD
will renew their strength.
They will soar on wings like eagles;
they will run and not grow weary,
they will walk and not be faint.*

ISAIAH 40:31 NIV

When our relationships are born
in the heart of God, they bring out the best
in us, for they are nurtured by love.

DON LESSIN

God is **listening** and **working** with you. I pray you see His **miraculous** work in your life and your friendships.

He redeems me from death and crowns me with love and tender mercies. He fills my life with good things.

PSALM 103:4–5 NLT

Nothing binds one human being to another more than the sense that they have been deeply, carefully listened to. It is no accident that we speak of paying attention to people; attention is the most valuable currency we have.

John Ortberg

I'm praying God's LOVE will overwhelm you today. He made you on PURPOSE with a PURPOSE. I thank God for you!

O give thanks to the LORD,
for He is good;
for His steadfast love
endures forever.

PSALM 107:1 NRSV

You were prescribed and then presented to this world exactly as God arranged it.

CHARLES SWINDOLL

God hears you. He knows your **generous** heart. He **loves** you. I'm praying His love will **multiply** your joys today.

How many are your works, O LORD!
In wisdom you made them all;
the earth is full of Your creatures.

Psalm 104:24 NIV

People who deal with life generously and large-heartedly go on multiplying relationships to the end.

ARTHUR CHRISTOPHER BENSON

You are such an

ENCOURAGEMENT

to me. You love God
and love others
so well!

*If I had such faith that I could move mountains,
but didn't love others, I would be nothing.*

I CORINTHIANS 13:2 NLT

I cannot count the number of times
I have been strengthened by another's
heartfelt hug, appreciative note, surprise gift,
or caring questions.... My friends are
an oasis to me, encouraging me to go on.
They are essential to my well-being.

Dee Brestin

Today, I prayed God would let His LIGHT beam through you for all the WORLD to see, even to those who don't want to see it.

We always pray for you, and we give thanks to God, the Father of our Lord Jesus Christ.

COLOSSIANS 1:3 NLT

Every day at work, home, school, and play, God presents us with opportunities to be a blessing to people who may not be as nice to us as we deserve or desire. In the middle of these opportunities He strengthens us and enables us to pay back good for evil.

THELMA WELLS

If kindness is contagious,
I'll surely catch it from you!
You do God's work
quietly and faithfully.
I thank God for you
every day.

Be completely humble and gentle;
be patient, bearing with one another in love.
EPHESIANS 4:2 NIV

Eating lunch with a friend.
Trying to do a decent day's work.
Hearing the rain patter against the window.
There's no event so common but that God
is present within it, in hidden ways,
always leaving you room to recognize Him.

FREDERICK BUECHNER

What a gift you are to your friends. You **motivate**, **encourage**, and **bless** us. I'm praying the knowledge of that is very real to you today.

Let us think of ways to motivate one another to acts of love and good works.

HEBREWS 10:24 NLT

Our footing is surer when we know that someone accepts us as we are, someone has our best interests at heart, someone is always glad to see us, someone plans to stick around. There are few blessings like the blessing of a friend.

Emilie Barnes and Donna Otto

I'm praying God
will fill your HEART
with deep and lasting
PEACE, that He will
listen to you like you
listen to me.

Peace I leave with you;
My peace I give you.

JOHN 14:27 NIV

*A true friend is someone who listens to us
with real concentration and expresses
sincere care for our struggles and pains.
She makes us feel that something very deep
is happening to us.*

SISTER HELEN FEENEY

I pray you'll **enjoy** and **celebrate** each moment of this special day, alongside those who **love** you the most.

Thanks be to God for His indescribable gift!
II Corinthians 9:15 NIV

Friendship is born at that moment when one person says to another, "You too? I thought I was the only one."

C. S. LEWIS

You show your FRIENDSHIP in a million little ways. That's why I'm thanking God for you today!

To those who use well what they are given, even more will be given.

LUKE 19:26 NLT

Enjoy the little things. One day you will look back and realize that those little things were the most important things of all.

Anonymous

You love others WARMLY, KINDLY—like we really matter. Today, I asked God to wrap His LOVE around you like a warm blanket.

Keep on loving each other....
Do not forget to show hospitality
to strangers, for by so doing
some people have shown hospitality
to angels without knowing it.

Hebrews 13:1-2 NIV

Love is not about what we do but who we are,
convincing others of our love for them...
and about who loves us.

JACK FROST

I'm praying you'll see God's **transforming power** today. He can truly make beautiful things out of ashes.

After Job had prayed for his friends, the LORD restored his fortunes and gave him twice as much as he had before.

JOB 42:10 NIV

Your greatest pleasure is that which rebounds from hearts that you have made glad.

HENRY WARD BEECHER

I'm praying God will **fill** your **life** with an abundance of **blessings**, nonsensical, unbelievable, and over-the-top blessings.

Whoever covers an offense seeks love.

PROVERBS 17:9 ESV

God's love is unreasonable. After all, He gave what He loved most, His Son, for those who cared not at all. Can you imagine that kind of immense, intense love?

Patsy Clairmont

DaySpring

Whatever your need is TODAY, God has it covered. I'm asking Him to work out the many DETAILS of what you are facing moment by moment as only He can.

All creation is waiting eagerly for that future day when God will reveal who His children really are.

ROMANS 8:19 NLT

Time is a very precious gift from God— so precious that it's only given to us moment by moment.

AMELIA BARR

I'm thanking God for the **loyalty** you show and the **hospitality** you share. You are an **anchor** that keeps us steady and safe.

Cheerfully share your home with those who need a meal or a place to stay.

1 Peter 4:9 NLT

We are all travelers in the wilderness of this world, and the best that we find in our travels is an honest friend.

ROBERT LOUIS STEVENSON

God is the heart
of any friendship, and I'm
THANKING HIM
for being at the heart
of ours.

Be devoted to one another in love.
Honor one another above yourselves.

ROMANS 12:10 NIV

Once the realization is accepted that even between
the closest human beings infinite distances
continue to exist, a wonderful living side by side
can grow up, if they succeed in loving the distance
between them which makes it possible for each
to see the other whole against the sky.

Rainer Maria Rilke

I'm PRAYING you'll release all your concerns to God's MIGHTY HAND and walk in His PEACE today.

My command is this:
Love each other as I have loved you.
John 15:12 NIV

How far you go in life depends on you being tender with the young, compassionate with the aged, sympathetic with the striving, and tolerant of the weak and the strong— because someday in life you will be all of these.

GEORGE WASHINGTON CARVER

I'm praying you'll trust Him to guide you through this. Friendships take work and dedication. I'm promising **to keep praying,** as long as it takes.

And Elijah said to Elisha, "Stay here...."
But Elisha replied, "As surely as the LORD lives
and you yourself live, I will never leave you!"

II KINGS 2:2 NLT

If a man does not make new acquaintances, as he advances through life, he will soon find himself left alone. A man...should keep his friendship in constant repair.

SAMUEL JOHNSON

Jesus knows exactly
how you feel and He is filled
with **compassion** for you.
I'm praying you'll find
kindness, wisdom,
and comfort through His
embrace today.

Walk with the wise and become wise.

PROVERBS 13:20 NIV

I expect to pass through life but once.
If, therefore, there can be any kindness
I can show, or any good thing I can do
to any fellow being, let me do it now...
as I shall not pass this way again.

William Penn

DaySpring

I asked God to work out the many details of what you're facing today. He KNOWS and He PROVIDES in His perfect way, in His perfect time.

They set out from their homes and met together by agreement to go and sympathize with him and comfort him.

JOB 2:11 NIV

Dare to love and to be a real friend. The love you give and receive is a reality that will lead you closer and closer to God as well as to those whom God has given you to love.

HENRI J. M. NOUWEN

DaySpring

Praying that every **moment** you've been there for others would be **returned** to you in blessings!

Do to others as you would like them to do to you.

Luke 6:31 NLT

Jesus wants to be our friend. He doesn't want us to walk alone. But it's not just that He wants us to be with Him; it's that He wants to be with us!

LEITH ANDERSON

Today I asked God to brighten your day with LOVE, JOY, AND FRIENDSHIP.

Love is patient and kind.

I CORINTHIANS 13:4 NLT

I wish you sunshine on your path and storms
to season your journey. I wish you faith—
to help define your living and your life.
More I cannot wish you—except perhaps love—
to make all the rest worthwhile.

Robert A. Ward

I'm praying you'll see God's LOVE all around you today. Be on the lookout for the KINDNESS and GOODNESS that are evidence of His love!

Therefore, as God's chosen people, holy and dearly loved, clothe yourselves with compassion, kindness, humility, gentleness and patience.
Colossians 3:12 NIV

We have been in God's thought from all eternity, and in His creative love, His attention never leaves us.
MICHAEL QUOIST

I asked God to steady
your heart and soul today,
and to give you joy, peace,
and hope during this time.
I prayed for His love
to surround you all day long.

*I am convinced that nothing can ever separate us
from God's love. Neither death nor life,
neither angels nor demons, neither our fears
for today nor our worries about tomorrow—
not even the powers of hell can separate us
from God's love.*

ROMANS 8:38 NLT

Love is always free to love, and arms
are always stretched as wide as the cross
toward anyone who needs to be loved.

EUGENIA PRICE

I'm praying you'll
fully embrace God's grace
and walk in the **freedom**
and **belonging** that is
yours in Christ Jesus.

*Use your freedom
to serve one another in love.*

GALATIANS 5:13 NLT

Being with you is like walking
on a very clear morning—
definitely the sensation
of belonging there.

E. B. White

I am HERE for you,
and I am PRAYING.
Today, I am praying
for God to give you
an ENDLESS supply
of blessings.

Never abandon a friend.

PROVERBS 27:10 NLT

Friendships need to be nurtured and guarded and fought for. We need to call one another without waiting to be called first. We need to ask how our friends are doing and really listen to their answers. Listen between the lines.

STASI ELDREDGE

I thanked God today
for giving us all fresh,
new **beginnings**.
I'm excited to see what
He has next for you.

Pray for each other....
The prayer of a righteous person
is powerful and effective.

James 5:16 NIV

I count your friendship one of the sweetest
things in my life, a comfort in time of doubt
and trouble, a joy in time of prosperity
and success, and an inspiration at all times.

EDWIN OSGOOD GROVER

You make me
a better person.
Praying you feel
VERY LOVED
and beautiful
today.

As iron sharpens iron,
so a friend sharpens a friend.

PROVERBS 27:17 NLT

A person who is given words of beauty
is a person who will express beauty....
All beauty can be traced, ultimately, to God.

Christopher de Vinck

You are **UNIQUELY** you, so different from me. But I thank God for the difference! We **COMPLEMENT** each other so well.

All of you together are Christ's body, and each of you is a part of it.

I Corinthians 12:27 NLT

You always grow to love the people you pray for. That's because you develop God's heart of love for them. Don't pass up the chance to experience that.

ANONYMOUS

I'm praying God
**will hold you
and protect you**
as you walk in the fullness
of His truth today.

*Love does not delight in evil
but rejoices with the truth.
It always protects, always trusts,
always hopes, always perseveres.*

1 CORINTHIANS 13:6-7 NIV

We all stumble, every one of us.
That's why it's a comfort
to go hand in hand.

EMILY KIMBROUGH

Today I asked the Lord to **help** you as much as you help me. You are always looking out for me. I cannot thank God enough for your **friendship.**

Don't look out only for your own interests, but take an interest in others, too.

PHILIPPIANS 2:4 NLT

It is the purest sign that we love someone if we choose to spend time idly in their presence when we could be doing something more constructive.

S. Cassidy

I'm praying for God to fill you with His **PERFECT PEACE** today. My prayers are always with you.

On Him we have set our hope that He will continue to deliver us, as you help us by your prayers.

II CORINTHIANS 1:10–11 NIV

For all of us, whether we walk old paths or blaze new trails, friends remain important.

LOIS WYSE

Today is a brand-new day that God has made just for you. I'm praying you'll find it to be **bright** and fresh and full of new, **exciting** beginnings. And that you have **confidence** in your potential!

This is the confidence we have in approaching God: that if we ask anything according to His will, He hears us.

1 John 5:14 NIV

A true friend prods you to personal growth, stretches you to your full potential. And most amazing of all, she celebrates your successes as if they were her own.

RICHARD EXLEY

Thank you for being an INDISPENSABLE part of my life. You are such a gift. I pray God pours His love over you today.

God has given each of you a gift from His great variety of spiritual gifts. Use them well to serve one another.

1 PETER 4:10 NLT

Friends are an indispensable part of a meaningful life. They are the ones who share our burdens and multiply our blessings.

Beverly LaHaye